S0-AYU-319

X-MOVES
Rally Car Dudes

by Michael Sandler

Consultant: Steve McCormick
NASCAR Expert and Writer

BEARPORT PUBLISHING

New York, New York

Credits

Cover and Title Page, © Lars Gange/Blackbullet.com; TOC, © Herbert Kratky/Shutterstock; 4, © Lars Gange/Blackbullet.com; 5, © Lars Gange/Blackbullet.com; 6, © Lars Gange/Blackbullet.com; 7, © Icon Sports Media; 8, © Bob Jackman and the Detroit Region SCCA (Sports Car Club of America); 9, © Tom Buchkoe; 10, Courtesy of JeremiÐ Aleksandar/jerra-codriver.com; 11, © Lars Gange/Blackbullet.com; 12, © Mark Sims/rallygallery.com; 13T, © Pete Kuncis/onalimbracing.com; 13B, © Lars Gange/Blackbullet.com; 14L, © Arthur Partyka/artpartphoto.com; 14R, © Ivy Pool; 15T, © Lars Gange/Blackbullet.com; 15B, © Lars Gange/Blackbullet.com; 16, © Juan Mabromata/AFP/Getty Images; 17, © Yiorgos Karahalis/Reuters/Landov; 18L, © Universal/Photofest; 18R, © Ethan Miller/Getty Images; 19, © Nate Christenson; 20, © Patrick Hertzog/AFP/Getty Images; 21L, © Claire Soares/Reuters/Landov; 21R, © Damien Meyer/AFP/Getty Images; 22T, © Lars Gange/Blackbullet.com; 22BL, © Natalia Siverina/Shutterstock; 23BC, © Christian Petersen/Getty Images; 23BR, © Grazia Neri/Getty Images.

Publisher: Kenn Goin
Senior Editor: Lisa Wiseman
Creative Director: Spencer Brinker
Photo Researcher: Jennifer Bright

Library of Congress Cataloging-in-Publication Data

Sandler, Michael.
  Rally car dudes / by Michael Sandler.
     p. cm. — (X-moves)
  Includes bibliographical references and index.
  ISBN-13: 978-1-59716-948-6 (library binding)
  ISBN-10: 1-59716-948-X (library binding)
  1. Rally cars—Juvenile literature. 2. Automobile rallies—Juvenile literature. I. Title.
  TL236.4.S36 2010
  796.72—dc22

                          2009015032

For more information, write to Bearport Publishing Company, Inc., 101 Fifth Avenue, Suite 6R, New York, New York 10003. Printed in the United States of America.

10 9 8 7 6 5 4 3 2 1

Contents

Racing for the Gold

Travis Pastrana and Colin McRae were both hungry for the victory. Each driver wanted the prize badly—the very first **X Games** rally-car gold medal. Travis, a young **motocross** champion, had just switched to rally car racing. Colin, a rally car **legend**, had won dozens of European races. After two days of speeding through the California desert, Travis and Colin were far ahead of all the other racers.

Now it was time for the final part of the race—a **super special stage** held in a Los Angeles stadium. Who would win—Travis or Colin?

Colin McRae ready to race at X Games 12 in 2006

4

Travis Pastrana speeding through one of X Games 12's desert stages

In addition to racing rally cars during X Games 12, Travis also competed in the Moto X Best Trick event and landed a double backflip to win the gold medal.

A Furious Flip

In the super special stage, racers take turns driving the course. Travis went first. He skidded around the tight corners—dirt flying behind his wheels—and finished with an incredible time. Next came Colin. Could he drive the course faster? Yes! He headed into the final jump one second ahead of Travis's time.

Colin flew over the jump cleanly. However, on landing, the left front wheel of his car got stuck in the dirt, ripping off the tire. The whole car flipped upside down and then completely rolled over. Finally, with the car settled back down on four wheels, Colin drove across the finish line. Still, the flip had cost him nearly a minute and the win. Travis won the gold!

Travis Pastrana with his X Games gold medal

6

Colin's car flips over at X Games 12.

Sadly, the great racing career of Colin McRae was cut short a year after the 2006 X Games. In 2007, he died in a helicopter accident near his home in Lanark, Scotland.

Rally Car Racing

Most car races take place in one afternoon on smoothly paved oval tracks. Rally car races are very different. They last several days and include a series of timed races called stages.

The stages are usually run on rough dirt tracks or unpaved roads in the desert, the woods, or the countryside. Drivers must handle rocks and boulders, dirt and mud, even snow and ice.

During a stage, drivers don't compete at the same time as they often do in other car races. Instead, each driver races alone against the clock, trying to complete the stage in the shortest time possible. The one who completes all the stages in the least total amount of time wins the rally.

Rallying isn't a new sport. The "Press On Regardless" rally in Michigan began in 1949.

8

American rally car racer Pat Moro races through the woods at the 2008 Lake Superior Pro Rally.

A race may have 8, 12, or even 20 stages. Usually, each stage is 15 to 20 miles (24 to 32 km) long.

A Team Sport

Most auto races take place on oval tracks where every lap is the same. In rallies, however, the drivers speed along unfamiliar roads. These roads are filled with steep hills, **hairpin turns**, and many other hazards.

Without help, a driver would have to go slowly. Driving fast would be too dangerous, and it would be easy to get lost. For these reasons, it takes two to rally: a driver and a co-driver.

The co-driver looks at maps and notes to see what lies ahead, checking the **odometer** to keep track of the miles. The driver can focus on going as fast as possible—up to 120 miles per hour (193 kph). He or she knows that the co-driver will give warning of any upcoming dangers.

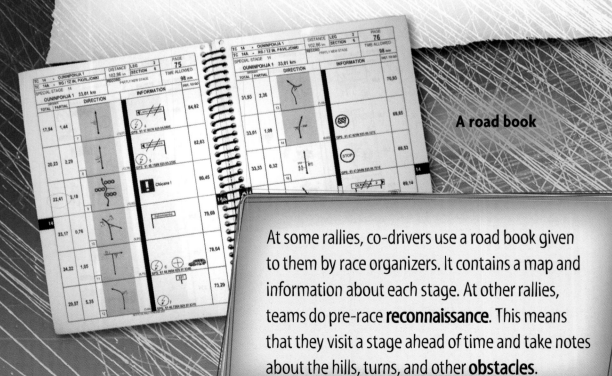

A road book

At some rallies, co-drivers use a road book given to them by race organizers. It contains a map and information about each stage. At other rallies, teams do pre-race **reconnaissance**. This means that they visit a stage ahead of time and take notes about the hills, turns, and other **obstacles**.

10

Driver Ken Block (right) and his co-driver Alex Gelsomino (left) at the Lake Superior Rally in 2008

11

The Rally Cars

Rally cars are a lot like regular cars, though they have a few important **modifications**. The tires, wheels, and **suspension systems** are extra tough to handle rugged rally roads. Skid plates beneath the cars protect the underbody from **ruts**, stumps, and rocks.

Inside, there aren't any cup holders or drop-down DVD players. Instead, there are **roll bars**, special racing seats, and harnesses to protect the driving team. Extra **gauges** on the dashboard let drivers carefully **monitor** their engines.

It's noisy driving at high speeds, so each car is equipped with headsets and microphones. Using them, drivers and co-drivers can always hear each other speak.

Rally cars are "street legal." Unlike special race cars used in Formula 1 or Indy car racing, they can be driven legally on ordinary streets.

12

Amy BeberVanzo and her Subaru Impreza WRX

Amy BeberVanzo, America's top female driver, races in a Subaru Impreza WRX. Along with the Mitsubishi Lancer Evo X, it's one of the most popular rally car models.

Rally America

America's most popular rally car race is Rally America. This set of nine races runs from January to October and determines the U.S. national rally car champion. The first race is Sno*Drift, a winter rally that takes place in Michigan. In freezing cold weather, drivers speed across icy, gravel roads trying not to **spin out** or get stuck. The series moves on to races such as Washington's Olympus Rally, Missouri's 100 Acre Wood, and the Ojibwe Forest Rally in Minnesota.

Travis Pastrana and Ken Block are often found battling for first place in Rally America events. At the 2008 Ojibwe race, Travis was the winner. Ken held a 19-second lead going into the final stage, but he flew off the road and crashed into a tree. Luckily, he wasn't hurt.

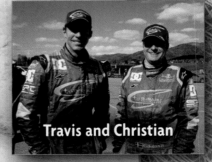

Travis Pastrana and his co-driver Christian Edstrom won the 2009 Sno*Drift rally.

Travis and Christian

Travis Pastrana has won the Rally America championship three times, most recently in 2008.

14

Ken Block

Ken Block took first place in the 2008 Olympus Rally by tying or winning 12 of the race's 16 stages.

World Rally Championship

The Europe-based World Rally Championship (WRC) is the biggest rally race series on the planet. The 12 WRC rallies take place in countries around the world—Ireland, Norway, Japan, even Australia. In recent years, French driver Sébastien Loeb has **dominated** the series.

Sébastien is a master at driving in all types of conditions. He speeds over the smoothly paved roads of Spain's Rally Catalunya in the fall. He flies over snow and ice at Rally Norway, during the bitterly cold winter. He is unfazed by the dusty roads and the searing heat at Greece's Acropolis Rally each summer. In all, Sébastien has won more than 50 WRC races.

Sébastien Loeb

16

Sébastien Loeb takes a curve during the Acropolis Rally in Greece in 2006.

On the dusty mountain roads of the Acropolis Rally, the temperature inside a car can soar to more than 120°F (49°C).

17

X Games

Since 2006, when the X Games added rallying to its extreme sports lineup, the event has drawn top racers from both America and Europe. One of them is Tanner Foust. Tanner is also a Hollywood **stunt driver**—he did the death-defying stunts in the movies *The Fast and the Furious: Tokyo Drift* (2006) and *The Bourne Ultimatum* (2007). In 2007, Tanner took the X Games gold, edging out Ken Block by less than a second.

At X Games 14 in 2008, Travis Pastrana returned to the top. He dedicated his gold medal to Colin McRae who had died the previous summer.

A scene from *The Fast and the Furious: Tokyo Drift*

Tanner Foust

Tanner Foust (left) and Ken Block (right) pull away at the start of X Games 13's final round in 2007.

In 2007, the X Games became extra exciting when it changed to a head-to-head format. This means that two racers start at the same time on **parallel** tracks. This format makes it easy to see who is going faster.

The Most Dangerous Rally

Rally car dudes are a wild breed of racers. They drive over rough roads in extreme conditions with little idea of what lies ahead. All rally car racers are tough, but Dakar drivers are the toughest.

The 5,000-mile (8,047-kph) Dakar Rally usually runs through the mighty Sahara Desert. Drivers begin in Europe—often Paris, France—and head south. Then they cross the sea by boat and race on to Dakar, Senegal, in Africa.

Towering dunes, camels, 140°F heat (60°C), and sand storms are just a few of the **hazards** drivers face in the Sahara. It sounds impossible, or nearly so, and that's just the way rally racers like it!

A driver passes a group of camels during a stage in the Dakar Rally.

20

Terrorists and desert bandits are two more dangers found in the Sahara. Due to these threats, the race is sometimes canceled or moved. The 2009 race, for example, was held in South America.

The Dakar rally has races for both cars and motorcycles. Stéphane Peterhansel, driving here, has won on a motorcycle six times and in a car three times.

Stéphane Peterhansel

21

Rally Car Racing 101

For rally car racing, drivers and co-drivers need special cars and protective gear to stay safe.

Racing Harness
These seat belts go over the shoulders and between the legs to keep drivers secure in their seats.

Driving Suit
They are fire resistant.

Lights
Lots of them are needed for when the roads are dark.

Wheels
Strong rims are needed for rough roads.

Car Body
It's raised higher than normal so it can ride over rocks and bumps.

Tires
Different types are used for different driving surfaces to provide the best traction on ice, snow, dirt, sand, gravel, or pavement.

Fire Extinguisher
If there's a crash, spilled gas can start a fire.

Roll Bars
These form a cage that protects the driving team in crashes or rollovers.

Headsets
They are used so the driver and co-driver can talk during races.

Helmets
Drivers and co-drivers always wear them to protect their heads.

22

Glossary

dominated (DOM-uh-*nay*-tid) held a superior position

gauges (GAYJ-iz) devices that display information about how a car is running

hairpin turns (HAIR-*pin* TURNZ) extremely sharp turns

hazards (HAZ-urdz) things that may be very dangerous

legend (LEJ-uhnd) someone who is very famous

modifications (*mod*-uh-fuh-KAY-shuhns) changes

monitor (MON-uh-tur) to keep track of, watch carefully

motocross (MOH-tuh-*kross*) a type of motorcycle racing

obstacles (OB-stuh-kuhlz) things that block a path

odometer (oh-DOM-i-tur) a device that measures the number of miles a car has traveled

parallel (PA-ruh-*lel*) running side by side

reconnaissance (rih-KAH-nuh-zinss) gathering of information about a place or event

roll bars (ROHL BARZ) steel bars in a car that create a protective cage for the people inside in case the car flips upside down

ruts (RUHTS) deep tracks made in the ground by wheels

spin out (SPIN OUT) to skid off the road

stage (STAYJ) one in a series of short races that make up a complete rally

stunt driver (STUHNT DRIVE-ur) a person who takes the place of an actor in a movie to perform difficult driving tricks

super special (SOO-pur SPESH-uhl) a type of rally car race that begins and finishes inside a stadium instead of in the backcountry

suspension systems (suh-SPEN-shuhn SISS-tuhmz) parts of a car that work to reduce the shock of riding over bumps and rough surfaces

terrorists (TER-ur-ists) nongovernment groups or people that use violence and terror to get what they want

X Games (EKS GAMEZ) an extreme sports competition held every year

23

Bibliography

Gifford, Clive. *Racing: The Ultimate Motorsports Encyclopedia*. Boston: Kingfisher (2006).

Los Angeles Times

rally-america.com

Read More

Savage, Jeff. *Rally Cars (Wild Rides)*. Mankato, MN: Capstone (2004).

Von Finn, Denny. *Rally Cars (Torque: Cool Rides)*. New York: Children's Press (2008).

Zuehlke, Jeffrey. *Rally Cars (Motor Mania)*. Minneapolis, MN: Lerner (2009).

Learn More Online

To learn more about rally car races, stars, and competitions, visit
www.bearportpublishing.com/X-Moves

Index